Bitcoin: Millionaire maker or Monopoly Money?

Contents

Introduction 3
Bitcoin's meteoric rise
Money – our global information system
Past, present and future monetary systems
Can Bitcoin be seen as a new asset class?

Crypto Currencies 5
The Root of all possibilities?

Understanding the Basics 6
What is Bitcoin?
The Background of Bitcoin
How is Bitcoin controlled?
Bitcoin Miners
Why do Bitcoins have value?
How do you spend or trade bitcoins?
3 ways you can acquire Bitcoin

Bitcoin Security & Transparency 14
Wallets: Online and offline
Is Bitcoin really anonymous?
Bitcoin addresses
BitCoin Fraud and Cyber Attacks:
eBay, Pyramid & Ponzi Schemes, Pump & Dump, 51% attacks

Bitcoin as an investment 21
Is Bitcoin in bubble territory?
Gold Versus Bitcoin
Bitcoin volatility
Bitcoin as an inflation hedge
The Bullish point of view
The Bearish point of view
The Bull versus The Bear
Where can investors buy Bitcoin?
Bitcoin funds for retail investors
Five phases of Bitcoin
Should you buy Bitcoin as an investment?

Will Bitcoin Survive? 31
Alternative Currencies from the past
Competitor digital currencies: Ripple, Litecoin, BQQ, PPCoin, DevCoin, NameCoin

Summary 35

Appendix 36
Technical mining information
Mining Pools
Bitcoin Mining Hardware
Bitcoin mining toolmakers
Useful Links

Disclaimer:
Unless specifically stated otherwise, any information contained in this e-book is for information purposes only and is not intended to be financial advice as it has been prepared without taking into account your financial objectives, financial situation or needs.

Introduction

Bitcoins meteoric rise

Bitcoin (BTC) came to my attention about 3 years ago. At that time it was still very much a niche product in a field dominated by computer geeks. It remained in my peripheral vision until mid 2013. Up until then I had viewed from the side lines like many other people and seen Bitcoin start its meteoric rise in price.

The mainstream financial institutions did not take Bitcoin seriously and they watched bemused as the price of a Bitcoin rose from $13 at the start of 2013 to over $1,000 in November of 2013. The original geeks that bought Bitcoin for a few dollars just a couple of years ago are now sitting on fortunes! No wonder everyone wants to find out what Bitcoin is!

This eBook explains what it is and explores how to use it and trade it. The million dollar question is: Has it got the potential to usher in a paradigm shift in our monetary systems? Because, if it does just a few pounds, euros, yen or dollars invested in it today could make you a millionaire in the future!

Money – our global information system

Money is our most pervasive global information system. It percolates through billions of daily exchanges in all strata of society around the World. The most important of our economic information systems - our money system, excludes millions of people who do no hold a bank account or credit card.

The architecture of our current banking and monetary system is inherited from the Victorian era. It is now inadequate for the challenges facing us during the Cyber Age. Bitcoin and other digital currencies could be part of the solution. For example: an expat worker in Saudi Arabia sending money home to India currently has to go through a convoluted transaction, at great cost, to send money to relatives. Bitcoin has the potential to totally revolutionise and democratise this type of transaction. The money could be sent for a negligible fee via Bitcoin between two smartphones or computers.

If Bitcoin can capture just a small fraction of this remittance market then the sky is the limit. If it can take just 5% market share from Gold, one Bitcoin could be worth over $37,000 in the future! However, many attempts at money reform have failed in the past. Will Bitcoin join the failures? This is just one of the many questions I look at in this eBook.

Past, present and future monetary systems

My career has taken me to the four corners of the World, where I have experienced extremely different situations ranging from dire poverty and hunger to immense affluence and extravagance.

As an asset manager I have invested money from a professional, hyper-rational angle. But it is also important to look outside the box at newly emerging technologies. Writing this eBook on Bitcoin has challenged some long held views I had about our current monetary systems. After all, our national currencies are just an agreed perception of value. They are no longer backed by gold. They are rectangular pieces of paper printed with many coloured designs!

During the course of this eBook you will discover some fascinating alternative currencies from the past plus glean insight into our present and future monetary systems.

Can Bitcoin be seen as a new asset class?

All aspects of the International money system interest me. As I am most involved with investing, there is a sizeable segment of this ebook devoted to whether Bitcoin should be considered as an alternative asset class. In the past year it has proved to be an outstanding investment – returning over 700%. Will this prove to be just hype and a bubble or could Bitcoin really be sustainable as an investment over the longer term? I have spent a lot of time looking at the pros and cons from an investing perspective. At times in the past I have held gold in my own portfolio and that of my clients. Now I ponder whether it is time to hold some Bitcoin as a hedge against inflation instead of gold. I share my conclusions on this subject with you later on.

Crypto Currencies

The Root of all possibilities?

The fact that changes in money systems are increasingly possible during an information revolution should come as no surprise. Money is modern society's central information system, rather like the nervous system in our own bodies. Mutations in a nervous system are relatively rare but when they occur they are very important events in the evolution of a species. Likewise, a change in the nature of our money system has the potential to facilitate a fundamental shift in our societies. Will Bitcoin and a host of other crypto currencies revolutionise our monetary systems?

A remarkable variety of non-conventional currencies have already been introduced over the last few decades. Some have become assimilated into the mainstream like frequent flyer air miles and store credits. Just a decade ago people were wary of Paypal but today it is well and truly accepted as a payment system. Paypal's market is now worth in excess of $22 billion!

The number of online and offline merchants accepting bitcoins grows with each passing day. Gaming company Zynga just announced it would accept Bitcoins. You can now buy a pizza on a site that's set up to take bitcoin payments or you can donate money to a church. Reddit, Wordpress, Foodler, and dating site OKCupid have all started accepting Bitcoins. Richard Branson's Virgin Galactic accepts Bitcoin and thereis already a Bitcoin ATM in Vancouver and another one planned for Hong Kong. Even Paypal is looking at ways to integrate Bitcoins into its payment network.

"Virtual currency is something that's here to stay," said eBay Inc. and Paypal Chief Executive John Donahoe.

Understanding the Basics

What is Bitcoin?

Bitcoin is a digital currency. It is money controlled and stored entirely by computers spread across the internet. Bitcoin is operated by a decentralized network of computers that anyone can join. Hence, it is a radically different to our existing monetary system. Instead of having one central authority which secures and controls the money supply (which most governments do for their national currencies), this work is spread out across the network via individual or "pools" of computers called miners.

Bitcoin is a transferable currency which is powered by an open source cryptographic protocol. However, Bitcoin is not just a currency, like pounds, dollars, euros or yen. It is a way of making payments, like PayPal or credit cards. It lets you hold money but it also lets you spend it and trade it. You can also move it from place to place, almost as cheaply and easily as sending an email. Bitcoin facilitates all of this without revealing your identity. In fact, some people would go as far as to say that Bitcoin is a re-imagining of international finance. Something that breaks down barriers between countries and frees currency from the control of federal governments. Bitcoin is also considered a peer to peer electronic cash system.

Because Bitcoin is not managed by a central authority, this also means that to date, it has no governance or regulation either.

Bitcoin has evolved from an obscure digital currency that hackers used to buy online products. It is now a robust, versatile online currency that anyone can use to buy online and offline products, trade or increase their business sales potential. Its uses are growing by the day and it is rapidly gaining mainstream acceptability.

The Background of Bitcoin

Bitcoin was developed in 2008 by an anonymous programmer or group of programmers going under the name of Satoshi Nakamoto. They built the Bitcoin software system and released it onto the internet. This was something that was designed to run across a huge network of computers, called bitcoin miners. The idea being that anyone could operate one of these machines. This open source, distributed software seeded the new currency, creating a small number of bitcoins. In essence, bitcoins are just long digital addresses and balances, stored in an online ledger called the "blockchain." The Bitcoin system was also designed so that the currency would slowly expand and so that people would be encouraged to operate as a bitcoin miner and therefore keep the system growing.

How is Bitcoin controlled?

Bitcoin is controlled by open source software that operates according to the laws of mathematics. There are people (the miners) around the world who collectively oversee this software. The software runs on thousands of machines across the globe. It can be changed only if a concensus of those overseeing the software agree to the change. The software operators are called miners.

Bitcoin Miners

From the start, the people running the computers that solve the mathematical problems were compared to gold miners digging the gold out of the ground so that everyone could use it. In reality Bitcoin "miners" are just running computer programs on very specialised hardware that automates the process of securing the network.

Miners collect the transactions on the network into large bundles called **blocks**. These blocks are strung together into one continuous, authoritative record called the **block chain**, which doesn't permit any conflicting transactions. This is necessary because without it people would be able to sign the same bitcoins over to two different recipients. Rather like writing cheques for more money than you have in your account! The block chain lets you know exactly which transactions count and can be trusted. One of the unique things about Bitcoin is that every transaction on its network is publicly available for anyone to examine. Any time a user sends a payment to another user, that transaction is reflected in the **block chain.** This is a permanent ledger of Bitcoin transactions.

You can examine every Bitcoin transaction that has ever occurred at a site called blockchain.info Here is a screenshot of what the **block chain** looks like.

Bitcoin: Millionaire maker or Monopoly Money?

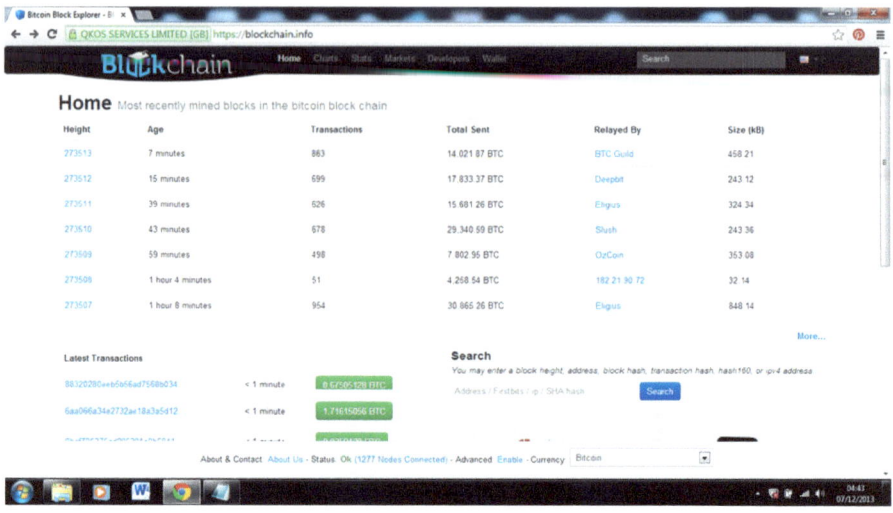

The way Bitcoin makes sure there is only one block chain is by making blocks really hard to produce. Miners have to compute a cryptographic hash of the block that meets certain criteria. Bitcoiners refer to this process as **"hashing"**. The only way to find a cryptographic hash that's good enough to count is to compute a whole stack of them until you get lucky and find one that works. Miners who successfully create a block are rewarded with some bitcoins according to a preset schedule. The difficulty of the criteria for the hash is continually adjusted based on how frequently blocks are appearing, so more competition equals more work needed to find a block. Nowadays a miner will need to try hundreds of millions of hashes per second. So to be competitive in this race miners need specialised hardware that can cost thousands of dollars. Running these mining rigs (as they are called) can be very costly due to the energy used 24/7. Mining was initially supposed to be a democratized thing, but now its becoming increasingly exclusive.

As the computing power required to mine Bitcoin increases exponentially, the revenue per mining operation is decreasing compared to mining operations just a few years ago. See the illustration below:

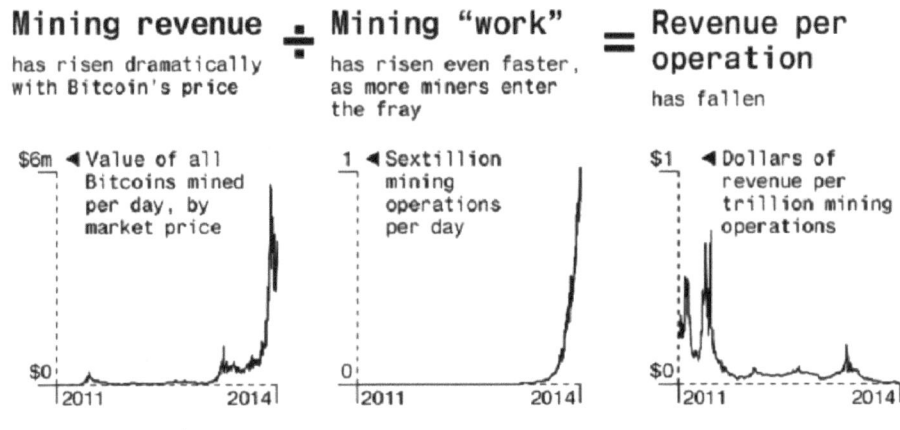

GRAPHIC BY BLOOMBERG BUSINESSWEEK.
DATA: BLOCKCHAIN.INFO

The other main task for miners is to carefully validate all the transactions that go into their blocks, otherwise they won't get any reward for their work!

It is this intense work that goes into finding blocks through hashing that secures the network against fraud. There is also, of course, much more nifty code that figures out things like how to choose between conflicting transactions and what to do if two people find valid blocks at the same time! A lot goes on behind the scenes at Bitcoin!

Summary of what Bitcoin Miners do:

Miners:

- Collect transactions from the network
- Validate transactions and don't allow conflicting ones
- Put transactions into large bundles called **blocks**
- Compute cryptographic hashes over and over until they find one "good enough to count"
- Submit the block to the network, adding it to the **block chain** and earning a reward in return.

*See the appendix for more technical information on Bitcoin mining and Bitcoin hardware.

Why do Bitcoins have value?

Since 2008, Bitcoin has evolved into something that a lot of people want to exchange, hoard as an investment or use to buy things with. The supply of Bitcoin is limited. So on a supply and demand basis the current demand is outstripping the supply. This is why the price has been rising rapidly.

Although the current system continues to produce bitcoins, this will stop when it reaches 21 million - in approximately the year 2140. The idea was to create a currency whose value couldn't be diminished by some central authority. When the Bitcoin system stops making new money, the value of each bitcoin will rise as demand rises, this is what is known as a deflationary currency. This is a currency whose value can't be watered down by some central authority, like the Federal Reserve or Bank of England cranking up the printing presses!

Although the supply of coins will eventually stop expanding, it will still be relatively easy to spend, as Bitcoins can be broken into tiny pieces. Each Bitcoin can be divided into one hundred million units, called Satoshis, after the currency's creator.

How do you spend or trade bitcoins?

Bitcoin is a maths-based currency. This means that the rules that govern bitcoin's accounting are controlled by cryptography. In simple terms, if you own some bitcoins, you own a private cryptography key that's associated with an address on the internet that contains a balance in the public ledger.

The address and the private key allow you to make transactions. The internet address is something everyone can see. It looks like a really complicated email address for online payments. Something akin to this: 1DTAXPKS1Sz7a5hL2Skp8bykwGaEL5JyrZ.

If someone wants to send you bitcoins, they need your address. If you want to send your bitcoins to someone else, you need your address and their address. But you also need your private cryptography key. This is an even more complicated string of code that you use to authorize a payment.

Using the maths associated with these keys and addresses, the system's public network of peer-to-peer computers (the bitcoin miners) check every transaction that happens on the network. If the maths doesn't add up, the transaction is rejected. The system so far has shown to be pretty secure.

3 ways you can acquire Bitcoin

1) Purchase Bitcoin

As an individual looking to acquire some Bitcoin, the first thing to do is to get a wallet. Many apps are available that you can download to your smart phone, tablet or laptop.

Once you have a wallet, you need some bitcoins. There are many places where an investor can buy Bitcoin or even a fraction of one, including Bitstamp and Coinbase. You do not have to invest large amounts of money - the minimum purchase at Coinbase for example is only 10 cents!

In the U.S. there are websites like Coinbase. For a 1% fee, Coinbase links to your bank account and then acts as a proxy for you, buying and selling bitcoins on an exchange. There are many such sites available around the world. They will all also offer an easy-to-use wallet. You can make much larger bitcoin purchases on big exchanges like Bitstamp, but to trade on these exchanges, you need to first send them cash. If you use a service like Coinbase or Mt. Gox, you'll have to provide a bank account and identification. But other services, such as LocalBitcoins, let you buy bitcoins without providing personal information. Ironically, the best way to do this is to meet up with someone in the real world and make the trade in-person. LocalBitcoins will facilitate such meetups, where one person provides cash and the other then sends bitcoins over the internet.

Alternatively you can attend a regular Bitcoin meetup in your part the world. Because credit card and bank transactions are reversible and bitcoin transactions are not, you need to be very careful if you're ever selling bitcoins to an individual.

BitCoins can also be purchased on eBay using PayPal or a credit or debit card. EBay and PayPal purchases can be risky as BitCoins are digital currency and as such, are not expressly covered by PayPal or eBay terms and conditions of service. PayPal's terms of service (at the time of writing) don't cover digital transactions. So, PayPal should not be used to buy non physical items.

When buying BitCoins, it is probably best to use a credit card. Credit Card companies tend to look after the best interests of their account holders and provide certain guarantees when it comes to all types of transactions.

The cautious should also opt to buy a prepaid Visa or MasterCard to complete the transaction. Prepaid cards are the least risky option because they are not linked to other accounts and do not provide any

information on the card holder. They also cannot be charged for more money than is on the card.
EBay tends to side with the buyer instead of the seller, so sellers are more at risk when using eBay to sell BitCoins. When it comes to buying BitCoins, it is up to the buyer to read all of the terms-of-service agreements and everything they can find out on the seller. It really still is Buyer Beware with Bitcoin!

2)Get paid in Bitcoin

BitCoins can be accepted as a payment by merchants and individuals who are willing to accept BitCoins in payment for a product or service.

How can I accept bitcoins in my business?

There are a number of ways one can go about accepting Bitcoin on a web interface. Keep in mind as you review these options that Bitcoin is still a young technology and many of these options aren't what you would call "user friendly" just yet. That said you do have quite a few options depending on your level of expertise and technical requirements:

Use a service like: BitcoinPayFlow or Bit-Pay

Use an existing shopping cart interface: There are existing plugins for Ubercart, Magento and many other popular e-commerce platforms. If you are looking to modify an existing site that happens to run on one of these platforms, this may be your best bet. If you've yet to start a site and don't want to write code yourself this may still be your best bet since you can choose your platform prior to implementation. Today,there are many online and offline retail establishments that accept BitCoins.

Early on in the Bitcoin story, the way of getting new bitcoins was to become a miner. That meant turning your computer into a bitcoin miner, becoming one of those nodes on Bitcoin's peer-to-peer network. Your machine would run the open source Bitcoin software.

As the price of bitcoins has shot up the mining game has become a commercial venture in itself. Professional players are in on the act with custom-designed hardware and rapidly expanding processing power requirements. It is no longer viable for the average person to mine Bitcoin. You would need to perform about 150 times as many mathematical operations as the world's most powerful supercomputer! And it is estimated that some Bitcoin miners now spend massive amounts per day on energy bills!

3) Mine Bitcoin

Mining is the only way to get **free** BitCoins. To mine Bitcoin nowadays an individual needs to own a computer with significant computing power and a high-end graphics card. This is because graphics cards are better designed to perform the complex algorithms needed to mathematically calculate the correct batch codes. Upon successful batch code creation, the miner will be awarded BitCoins. As of April 2013 some Bitcoin miners were supposedly consuming $150,000 per day in electricity! Hardly a viable hobby for most of us!

Bitcoin Security & Transparency

Bitcoin verifies transactions with the same state-of-the art encryption that is used in military and government applications.

Wallets

For ordinary people who use the Bitcoin network to buy, sell and exchange, managing addresses and keys can be daunting. Many different types of programs, called wallets have been designed, that keep track of all these bits of code for you. You can install a wallet on your computer or your mobile phone, or use one that resides on a website. With a wallet in place, you can then easily send and receive bitcoins via the internet. You can do all sorts of transactions from sending money to a relative abroad, buying goods or making a charitable donation.

As in real life, you must keep your wallet safe. Bitcoin makes it possible to transfer value anywhere quickly and easily, but therein lies the security concerns too. A Bitcoin wallet is like a wallet with cash. If you wouldn't keep a thousand dollars or pounds in your pocket, you might want to have the same consideration for your Bitcoin wallet.

In general, it is good practice to keep only small amounts of bitcoins on your computer, mobile, or server for everyday use and to keep the remaining part of your funds in a safer environment. Bitcoin can provide very high levels of security if used correctly (more on this later). Always remember that it is your responsibility to adopt good practices in order to protect your money.

Be careful with online services

Online wallets and exchanges look like online banks. However, you should always choose such services carefully. As of today, these services generally don't provide enough insurance and security to be used to store your money like a bank. Using security features like two-factor authentication can help to increase the security of your accounts. Instant transactions are less secure.

A Bitcoin transaction is usually deployed within a few seconds and begins to be confirmed in the following 10 minutes. During that time, a transaction can be considered authentic but still reversible. Dishonest users could try to cheat you. If you can't wait for a confirmation, asking for a small transaction fee or using a detection system for unsafe transactions can increase security. For larger amounts like $500 or more it makes sense to wait for 6 confirmations or more. Each confirmation exponentially decreases the risk of a reversed transaction.

Can you lose your wallet with Bitcoin in it?

BitCoin wallets can be deleted. So it is very important to make a backup of the wallet. If the wallet cannot be restored via a backup the BitCoins and associated addresses and private encryption keys in it, are lost forever. This is the primary way people lose their BitCoins and lessen the number of BitCoins in circulation.

Backup your wallet

Stored in a safe place, an encrypted backup of your wallet can protect you against computer failures and human error. It can also allow you to recover your wallet in the event that your mobile, tablet or computer is stolen. Some wallets use many hidden private keys internally. If you only have a backup of the private keys for your visible Bitcoin addresses, you might not be able to recover a great part of your funds with your backup. So, **backup your entire wallet.**

Encrypt online backups

Any backup that is stored online is highly vulnerable to theft. Any computer that is connected to the Internet is vulnerable to malicious software. So, encrypting any backup that is exposed to the network is vital for your security.

Use multiple secure locations

As any security expert will tell you - single points of failure are bad for security. If your backup is not dependent on a single location it is much more likely that you will be able to recover your wallet. You might also want to consider using different media types like USB keys, paper and CDs as ways of storing your backups.

You need to backup your wallet on a regular basis to make sure that all recent Bitcoin change addresses and all new Bitcoin addresses you created are included in your backup. Encrypting your wallet or your smartphone allows you to set a password for anyone trying to withdraw any funds. This helps protect against thieves, though it cannot protect against keylogging hardware or software.

Never forget your password

Make sure you never forget your password or your funds will be permanently lost. Unlike your bank, there are very limited password recovery options with Bitcoin. If you are saving Bitcoin as an investment, you will need to remember your password even after many years. You might want to keep a paper copy of your password in a safe place like a vault.

Make sure you use a strong password. Don't use recognizable words. A strong password should contain letters, numbers, punctuation marks and must be at least 16 characters long. The most secure passwords are those generated by programs designed specifically for that purpose. Strong passwords are of course much harder to remember, so you should take care in memorizing it.

Offline wallets

An offline wallet, also known as cold storage, provides the highest level of security for Bitcoin savings. It involves storing a wallet in a secured place that is not connected to the network. When done properly, it can offer a very good protection against computer vulnerability. Using an offline wallet in conjunction with backups and encryption is good security practice.

Bitcoin payments are irreversible

Any transaction issued with Bitcoin cannot be reversed. The only option is to get a refund from the the person receiving the funds. That means you should take care to do business with people and organizations you know and trust, or who have an established reputation. Business owners who accept Bitcoin should be aware of the payment requests they are displaying to their customers.

Unless you intend to receive public donations or payments with full transparency, publishing a Bitcoin address in any public space such as a website or on a social network is not a good idea. If you move any funds with this address to one of your other addresses, they will be publicly tainted by the history of your public address.

You should also be careful not to publish information about your transactions and purchases that could allow someone to identify your Bitcoin addresses.
Bitcoin can detect typo errors and usually won't let you send money to an invalid address by mistake. As Bitcoin becomes more mainstream, I am sure more choice and protection for the consumer will be forthcoming.

Is Bitcoin really anonymous?

In essence – no!
Bitcoin works with an unprecedented level of transparency that most people are not used to. All Bitcoin transactions are public, traceable, and permanently stored in the Bitcoin network.

Bitcoin addresses are the only information used to determine where bitcoins are allocated and where they are sent. These addresses are created privately by each user's wallet. But, once addresses are used they clearly record the history of all the transactions they have been involved in. Anyone can see the balance and all the transactions of any address on the blockchain.

Since users usually have to reveal their identity in order to receive physical services or goods, Bitcoin addresses cannot remain fully anonymous. For these reasons, Bitcoin addresses should only be used once and users must be careful not to disclose their addresses.

Your IP address can also be logged. As Bitcoin is a peer-to-peer network, it is possible to listen for transactions' relays and log their IP addresses. You might want to consider hiding your computer's IP address with a tool like Tor so that it cannot be logged.

Use a new Bitcoin address each time you receive a new payment

To protect your privacy, you should use a new Bitcoin address each time your receive a new payment. In addition, use multiple wallets for different purposes. Doing this allows you to isolate each of your transactions in such a way that it is not possible to associate them all together. People who send you money cannot see what other Bitcoin addresses you own and what you do with them. This is probably the most important advice to keep in mind.

Use change addresses when sending payments

You can use a Bitcoin client such as Bitcoin-Qt that makes it difficult to track your transactions by creating a new change address each time you send a payment. For example, if you receive 10 BTC on address A, and you later send 3 BTC to address B, the remaining change must be sent back to you. Some Bitcoin clients are designed to send the change to a new address C in such a way that it becomes difficult to know if you own Bitcoin address B or C.

Mixing Services

There are online services called mixing services that offer to mix traceability between users by receiving and sending back the same amount using independent Bitcoin addresses. The legality of using such services will vary and be subjected to different rules in each country. A mixing service also requires you to trust the individuals running them not to lose or steal your funds and not to keep a log of your requests. Even though mixing services can block traceability for small amounts, it becomes increasingly difficult for larger transactions.

Although Bitcoin has become know for its anonymity, infact some effort is required to protect your privacy with Bitcoin.

BitCoin Fraud and Cyber Attacks

eBay

There have been a few occurences of BitCoin fraud on eBay.
In these instances, the seller agreed to sell X amount of BitCoins to a buyer for a certain price. The buyer agreed to buy the BitCoins and sent their payment information. On eBay, sellers do not have to ship products until the buyer pays. This requires a lot of trust on the buyer's part.

The seller accepted the money but never made the BitCoins available to the buyer. In this instance, the buyer had to take up their case with eBay and with their payment provider. The outcome is unknown. This can be a long and often fruitless process.

The best way to avoid being scammed by an eBay seller is to review their rating and the reviews offered by other buyers. If there are a lot of complaints or the seller has a low rating or very few sales, DO NOT go ahead with the transaction and move on to a reputable seller.

Is BitCoin Pyramid selling or a Ponzi scheme?

BitCoin is not a Ponzi scheme (like Bernard Madoff) or a pyramid scheme. For something to be a Ponzi or a pyramid scheme, the initial members would have to gain money from the later users.

The founders and first users of BitCoin do not make a profit from the newer members, and they do not earn BitCoins by referring individuals to the BitCoin network. Some of the founding members of BitCoin have made a lot of money because of the increasing value of BitCoin, but this has not been at the expense of later Bitcoin users.

Is BitCoin a "pump and dump" scam?

There is some worry among programmers and developers that extremely new currencies could be used as "pump and dump" scams.

A "pump and dump" scam is where an individual or a group of individuals create an alternative currency, allocate themselves lots of coins, and then market it to unsuspecting users at a very rapid pace. The price of each individual coin increases rapidly and at the height of the increase, the original creators dump their coins and rake in massive profits. The rest of the available coins then plummet rapidly in value and become virtually worthless.

If Bitcoin was a "pump and dump" scam the original creators would likely have dumped their Bitcoin when it got to over $1,000 per Bitcoin back in November 2013.

To date, digital or crypto currencies remain largely unregulated. But as they become more popular this will definitely change.

Online cyber attacks

Danish bitcoin exchange Bips had to shut down its consumer wallet after suffering a major cyber-attack that saw £1 million in bitcoins stolen. Bips is one of the largest bitcoin exchanges in Europe.

There has been a string of raids conducted by cyber-criminals on bitcoin exchanges worldwide, as the soaring value of the virtual currency holds out the prospect of a bumper payoff for successful hackers.

Recently, hackers also breached security at a site called inputs.io — which stores bitcoins in digital wallets for people worldwide. Allegedly, they made off with about $1.2 million in bitcoins! Cyber attacks are a reality so many seasoned Bitcoin pros move their wallets off their computers and will save them on a thumb drive or other flash storage device that's not connected to the internet. Some people even move their bitcoins into a real physical wallet or onto something else that is completely separate from the computer world. They may write their private key on a piece of paper. Others will engrave their crypto key onto a ring or even onto a metal coin. Of course you could lose this. But the same goes for a paper note such as a $10 bill or a £10 note.

The good news is that the public nature of the bitcoin ledger may make it theoretically possible to figure out who has stolen your bitcoins. You can always see the address that they were shipped off to, and if you ever link that address to a specific person, then you've found your thief. In reality, this is an extremely complex process and researchers are only just beginning to explore the possibilities of tracing thieves.

What is a 51% attack?

The only way someone could steal BitCoins on a mass scale is if they successfully execute a 51% attack on the entire network.

This means that a single user would have to create a computer system with more processing power than 50% of the entire network. The odds of a successful 51% attack decrease with time because more and more individuals enter the network and start buying, selling, and transacting using BitCoins. Also, more miners enter the network, hoping to make a few free BitCoins, which makes the network bigger and the processing power greater.

Once an individual successfully executed a 51%, they would have to immediately start two more forks from a batch code. The first fork would have to route the transaction BitCoins to a place that either cashes BitCoins out for the local currency or stores the BitCoins undetected. The second fork would have to simultaneously continue the transaction as if nothing covert were happening. It is in this way that the unscrupulous miner would get BitCoins for solving numerous transaction codes and double spending BitCoins.

Nothing is impossible but successfully carrying out a 51% attack is highly improbable.

Bitcoin as an investment

Bitcoin has become a real phenomenon over the last few years. During 2013 alone its price has risen from around $13 to $1,000! There are not many stocks that can boast a chart like this one!

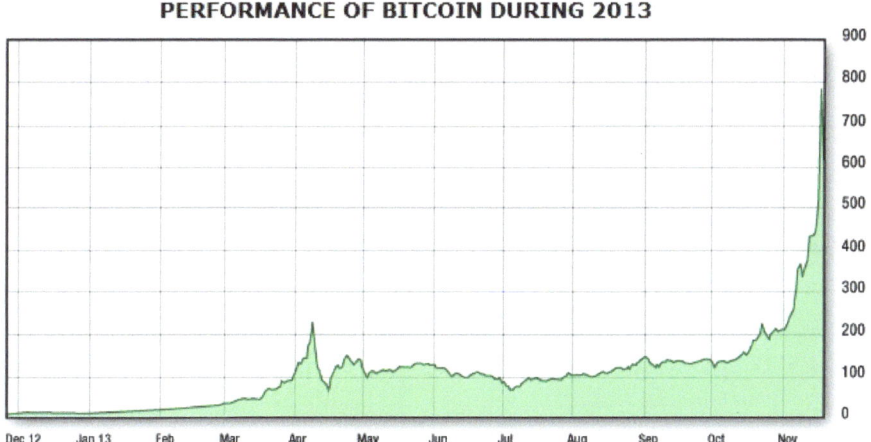

Is Bitcoin in bubble territory?

This chart does look like a bit of a bubble - akin to the great tulip bubble of the 1600s in Holland. The Tulip Bulb Mania was the rapid rise in price of tulip bulbs that had just been introduced into Holland. Tulip Mania mostly occurred in Holland but England and Germany did experience the mania to a lesser degree too. In 1636 tulips were publicly sold on the London Stock Exchange.

During the Tulip Bulb Mania people were speculating with tulip bulbs trying to make a quick profit. They never ever intended to plant the bulbs. They were purchased with the intention of selling them again for a higher price. Property, animals and money were all traded for tulip bulbs.

The bulbs were traded on local market exchanges. Some varieties of tulip bulbs were changing hands for more than the cost of a house in Amsterdam! Others cost more than 45 oxen!

Eventually the tulip market began to decline as some people began to liquidate their tulips bulbs and more bulbs were introduced into the supply. Quickly after this, there was a panic in which everyone started selling frantically. In less than 6 weeks the tulip prices crashed by over

90%. When the mania was over, the price of tulips dropped from a high of $76,000 to less than $1!

This is a scenario that is not impossible for Bitcoin. There are speculators in the Bitcoin market and there is currently no mechanisim in place to prevent speculators hoarding Bitcoin. If sentiment becomes bearish or punitive legislation is brought in, then panic selling could set in and the price could plummet.

Bitcoin is not yet defined as an asset - a commodity or a currency. But, if we accept that Bitcoin is an asset class in its own right, then it would have to be seen as an incredibly volatile one. Bitcoins are only worth something as long as other investors or merchants think they are. That has led some pundits to compare Bitcoins to gold as a "store of value." The longer Bitcoin persists, the more people will have faith in them as a legitimate store of value. After all, gold has been around a long time!

Gold Versus Bitcoin: 22% return versus 700% return respectively in 2013

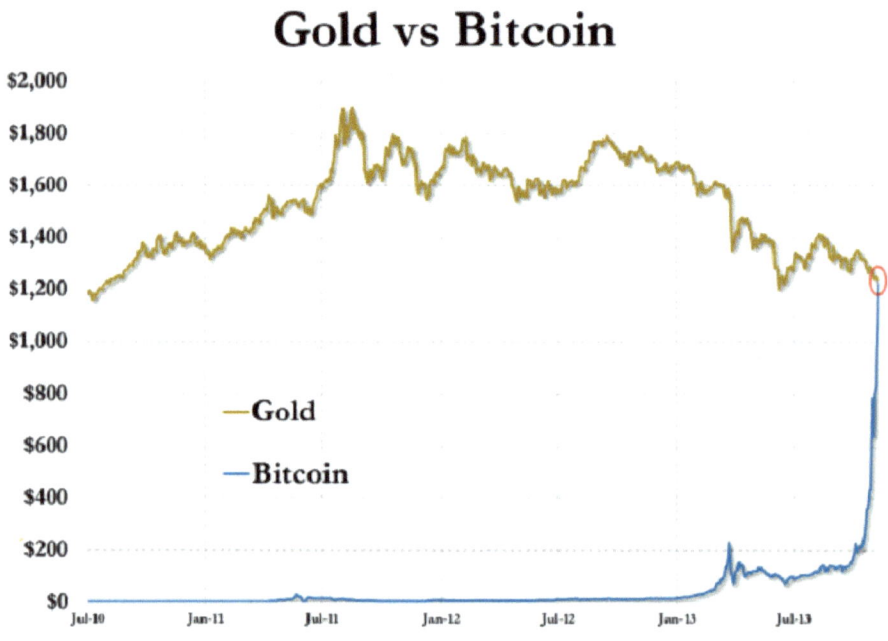

Bitcoin has totally outperformed Gold as an investment during 2013. However, if I am to play devil's advocate - it is still just another fiat currency (i.e. not backed by any real asset). Why buy a fiat currency after a +700% rise in a year, when you could buy a universally recognized commodity like gold, silver or platinum that has been a store of value for over 500 years? These commodities are all well off their highs whilst Bitcoin could be in bubble territory. With gold, silver and platinum there are also uses in jewelry and industrial applications. Gold's value can certainly be overstated at times, but it does have practical uses too. Bitcoin does not.

The Bitcoin price is volatile

According to an analysis of bitcoin prices performed for The Wall Street Journal between late 2010 and 2013, bitcoin's return in U.S. dollars had an annualized "standard deviation" of about 139%. That means that it was roughly 7½ times as volatile as gold and more than eight times as volatile as the S&P 500 index.

I consider gold and other precious metals as VERY volatile investments, but Bitcoin is even more volatile! The price of a bitcoin can increase and decrease rapidly over a short period of time. It is still a developing market with a novel nature, and sometimes the Bitcoin market is illiquid.

Consequently, I believe that keeping all your savings in Bitcoin would not be prudent at this point. Bitcoin should be seen as a high risk asset, and you should never store money that you cannot afford to lose in Bitcoin.

Bitcoin as an inflation hedge

Marie Brière, an associate professor at Université Paris Dauphine in France, calculated that between July 2010 and July 2013, bitcoin had an annualized return of more than 370% with 175% volatility. She found that its returns had a weak but significant correlation with gold and inflation-linked bonds, supporting the notion that some investors see bitcoin as an inflation fighter. Her research concluded that a small allocation to bitcoin perhaps 3% of a well-diversified portfolio could improve one's risk-reward trade-off. Below I will include the Pros and Cons from an investor's perspective and look at the Bulls versus Bears on the investment outcomes for Bitcoin.

The million dollar question for long term investors is: Does bitcoin really have a sustainable future?

The Bullish point of view

Investing in bitcoin is getting easier for those who have little understanding of its basics. That has been fantastic for speculators, as such demand has driven up the price, which fuels more interest, demand, and even higher prices. If Bitcoin can survive and thrive then the outlook for investors looks excellent. As Bitcoin prices powered through the $1,000 barrier in November 2013, some fantastic scenarios were being bandied about...

The founder of a Swedish political party believes that the Bitcoin market could capture between 1 to 10% of the total foreign exchange market. If that were to happen the value of each Bitcoin could go up to $100,000. If Bitcoin can capture just a small fraction of the remittance market then the sky is the limit. If investors start to consider it as a gold substitute and it can capture just 5% market share from Gold one Bitcoin could be worth over $37,000 in the future!

Bitcoin fills a niche of digital and frictionless exchange of value. While online purchases require the regular credit card authentication requirements of a billing address, Bitcoin can be used as easily as handing over cash. There is value in this. The table below illustrates a few bullish scenarios:

If Bitcoin Equals the Value of...	Basis for Comparison	Current Value	Implied Value Per Bitcoin
Western Union (NYSE: WU)	Money movement and transmittance platform	$11.5 billion	$966
PayPal	Leading online payment network	$22.8 billion	$1,916
Monetary base of Turkey	Emerging market currency	$95 billion	$7,983
5% of gold	Primary global store of value	$450 billion	$37,815

The Bearish point of view

There are plenty of Bitcoin sceptics, many of them being competitors in the money transfer and exchange market or economists who debate the value of money made from nothing but ones and zeroes! Western Union for instance has highlighted Bitcoin's lack of liquidity and adoption, the immature consumer interfaces and the regulatory issues that need to be addressed before it would be ready to compete with it in the international money transfer market.

However, new competition has already forced Western Union to lower prices, and as a result, its operating margins have fallen considerably. Western Union is "keeping an eye on further developments" with Bitcoin and other digital currencies. This implies that they are perceived as real threats in this sector.

Economist Paul Krugman, among many other critics who look back wearing the dour goggles of history, argue that it is just the latest speculative mania. Meanwhile, an industry of microprocessor manufacturers has sprung up to serve the Bitcoin miners and regardless of the fate of Bitcoin, one consequence of the race to mine it will probably be faster chips. The sceptics fear that an organization with heaps of capital and not much idealism can buy enough computational power to corner the market and price out the individual miner. Indeed, that may already be happening: Websites such as BitcoinWatch, that track the total computing power of miners have started to observe huge, mysterious spikes in capacity.

The Bull versus The Bear

Everytime the Bitcoin price increases then there are vested interests in keeping it around longterm. There are plenty of financial interests backing its success. For payment processors like Western Union and Paypal there is the opportunity to disrupt the current hegemony of credit card processors and banks. Partnering in some way with Bitcoin in this venture could be a better prospect than fighting Bitcoin's rise.

Regulation is the biggest unknown at this stage. State governments in the US take in 22% of their revenue from sales taxes - the largest source outside of transfers from the federal government. Protecting this would be in their best interest. Bitcoin payments attract no tax so far!

However, there seems to be encouraging rumblings from the Federal Reserve - they seem to understand its promise. In late 2013 Jennifer Shasky Calvery, the director of the Treasury Department's Financial Crimes Enforcement Network said that Bitcoin poses problems, but she also said that it's a bit like the internet in its infancy.

"So often, when there is a new type of financial service or a new player in the financial industry, the first reaction by those of us who are concerned about money laundering or terrorist finance is to think about the gaps and the vulnerabilities that it creates in the financial system," she said. "But it's also important that we step back and recognize that innovation is a very important part of our economy."

Bitcoin certainly can provide such innovation. It just may take a while longer for the rest of the world to completely catch on. Purely from an investment point of view, the uncertain regulatory environment adds further risk to investing in Bitcoin. Bitcoin's future is looking bright but there are still regulatory and liquidity obstacles to be overcome.

Comparing the search popularity on Google between gold and Bitcoin it looks like gold is still more widely searched but in recent months Bitcoin is starting to gain traction. More people have started searching for Bitcoin and as reports on mainstream news channels increase, so will Bitcoin searches. As awareness grows so will the number of transactions and the liquidity.

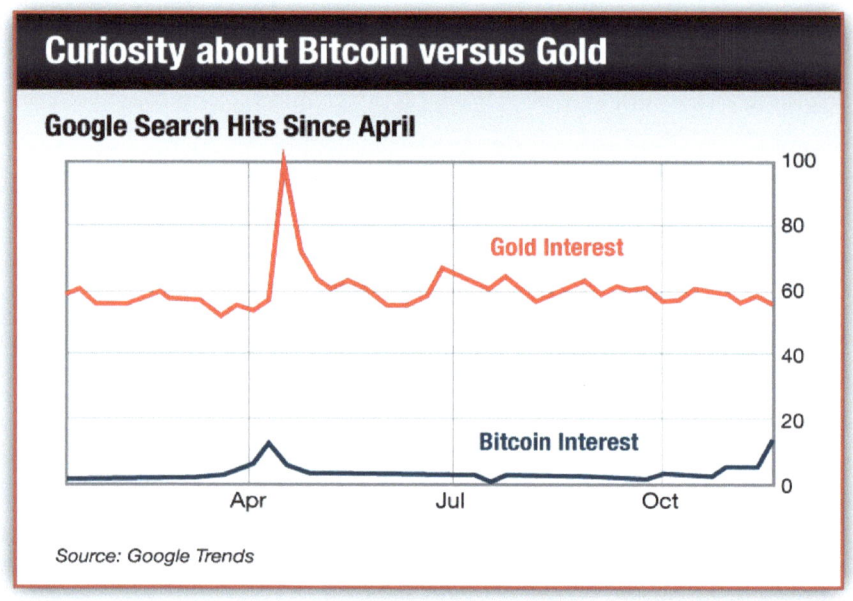

Where can investors buy Bitcoin?

There are many places where an investor can buy a Bitcoin or even a fraction of one, including Slovenia-based Bitstamp.net,Coinbase and eBay. For smaller investors the good news is that the minimum purchase at websites like San Francisco-based Coinbase is just 10 cents! Investors can also purchase bitcoins online through bigger operators such as the Tokyo-based Mt. Gox. Mt.Gox is the world's most established Bitcoin exchange. You can quickly and securely trade bitcoins with other people around the world with your local currency!

There's now a Bitcoin ATM in Vancouver and another one planned for Hong Kong. In addition, a number of alternative digital currencies have sprung up with names such as Litecoin and Peercoin, though none is remotely as popular as Bitcoin – yet!

Bitcoin funds are already being proposed for retail investors

Twins, Cameron and Tyler Winklevoss, famous for their battles with Facebook boss Mark Zuckerberg claim to hold about 1% of all Bitcoin mined so far - over $11 million worth! Other venture capital firms are investing in Bitcoin too.

The Winklevoss Bitcoin Trust will initially sell $20m (£13m) worth of shares to investors, according to a filing with the Securities and Exchange Commission to launch an exchange-traded fund, called the Winklevoss Bitcoin Trust. The Trust will hold Bitcoins and the value of the fund will closely track the value of the underlying Bitcoins. In an email from their lawyer, the Winklevosses said they are working with the SEC to finalize the proposal and hope to launch in 2014.

The twins said that shares in the trust were "designed for investors seeking a cost-effective and convenient means to gain exposure to Bitcoins with minimal credit risk". At this point we do not know which stock exchange it will be listed on. Presumably Nasdaq.
The intention is that investors will be able to sell shares in the trust fund short, in effect allowing them to speculate that the value of Bitcoins will fall. This will irritate the crypto currency's main demographic; people who are purposefully avoiding traditional banking. The whole point of Bitcoin is surely its independence and status as an alternative currency that is not designed to be used for pure speculation.

The SEC filing warned that as "the sponsor and its management have no history of operating an investment vehicle like the Trust, their experience may be inadequate or unsuitable to manage the Trust". Clearly they will have to appoint a mainstream financial institution to run the fund!

SecondMarket, launched an open - ended trust called the Bitcoin Investment Trust, which holds Bitcoins. Shares in the Trust bumped along for around two weeks after its launch on 26th September. Following this, they began creeping up, before beginning their rapid rise around 4th November. The Trust has been buying bitcoins from exchanges, merchants, individual users, and miners. SecondMarket CEO Barry Silbert says the trust, which is available in certain self-directed individual retirement accounts (IRAs), has attracted over $36 million in assets already.

For those that believe in the long term potential of Bitcoin on the timescale of decades, this exposure via an IRA could be a great opportunity...or not. This trust is designed for sophisticated investors looking for exposure to Bitcoin in a simple investment vehicle, without the confusing and cumbersome experience of buying, storing and safekeeping large quantities of bitcoins themselves.

For this convenience they charge 1.5% front load and back load with an additional 2% annual fee for administration and safekeeping. This trust provides larger investors with a compliance-assured method of investing in Bitcoin. Apparently Second market has around 90 investors so far and just over half a percent of all bitcoins mined to date. The minimum investment is $25,000.

As more companies launch retail type funds with Bitcoin as the undelying investment, it will increase awareness, make it more investible as an asset class and drive up the price even further by reducing supply.

The fact that self directed IRA providers like PENSCO, EnTrust, Equity Institutional, and Millennium Trust, are allowing Bitcoin Trusts as an investment option is indicative that the old style financial institutuions are already embracing Bitcoin as an investment with a future and trying to get in on the act!

Like any new invention there is a process of commercialization that has to take place before its investment potential can be realized. If Bitcoin can successfully negotiate the following five phases, then early investors could reap mega profits.

Five phases of Bitcoin

Phase 1 : The first phase of Bitcoin was driven by hobbyist hackers and computer geeks

Phase 2: In the second phase early adopters and technology entrepreneurs piled in.

Phase 3: In the third phase, portfolio managers, traders and bank executives started investing personally in Bitcoin. During 2013 venture capital companies started to take an interest and began building infrastructure on top of the protocol, which is currently designed for wealthier investors.

Phase 4: In phase four Wall Street and the traditional financial institutions will want a piece of the action.

Phase 5: By phase five, the general public will fully engage and adopt Bitcoin into the mainstream.

If phase five comes to fruition Bitcoin will revolutionize the way people deal with money, driving efficiencies into the process and potentially saving people money. But for that to happen, the first four stages are necessary to evolve the virtual currency and drive liquidity into the market.

Should you buy Bitcoin as an investment or avoid it like the plague?

The question for investors now is should you buy the crypto currency or avoid it?

Unlike traditional money, bitcoin exists only online. Over half of all the Bitcoin ever to exist have already been mined. Once the figure reaches 21 million their mining will stop. Its limited supply has made Bitcoin attractive to people worried about inflation and its anonymous nature makes it a favourite among those wanting to make anonymous transactions.

If Bitcoin can secure a small portion of the huge remittance market then its price will rise much further, but there's also a chance that it will go out of favour and become worthless. Like any speculative investment, if a disruptive technology breaks through to the mainstream the price of its stock can rocket, but if it flounders its stock price can plummet.

Some investors will treat it as a gold substitute having only a small exposure. It should definitely be classed as a "risky alternative" in the same vein as a hedge fund. At this stage in its development Bitcoin has to be seen as long-term speculation rather than a short-term trade or a long-term investment. View it as money that can be completely lost.

Some say that Bitcoin will either produce a total loss of principal or a very, very high return. Because of Bitcoin's all-or-nothing nature see it as a lottery ticket. Taking a tiny risk won't damage your portfolio if Bitcoin goes bust. But if Bitcoin really takes off it could have a life changing impact on the value of your investment portfolio.

As Bitcoin mania unfolds, the currency might turn out to be merely a speculative bubble that bursts just like the tulips did. Alternatively an investor willing to stake say 1-3% of their savings might be part of a success story that is life changing in its ability to generate huge profits.

Conservative and cautious investors

Bitcoin is an experimental new currency that is still in active development. Although it becomes less experimental as its usage grows, you should keep in mind that Bitcoin is a relatively new invention. Its future cannot be predicted by anyone. Conservative investors should certainly steer clear of Bitcoin, but for the more daring a handful of bitcoins could one day make you very rich!

Don't forget Tax

Bitcoins aren't useful as a way to avoid taxes—legally, at least. In the US, the Government Accountability Office recently stated that: income earned through virtual currencies is taxable. Some issues remain to be clarified, such as whether gains should be taxed in the same way as those from commodities or as collectibles. Infact most jurisdictions still require you to pay income, sales, payroll, and capital gains taxes on anything that has gained value, including Bitcoin.

Will Bitcoin Survive?

E-Gold and Digital Money Trust were created in the mid to late 1990s, and they are now both defunct. The exact reasons for their demise are not known. Though, it was probably because of lack of interest. BitCoin could go the same way but at the moment there is huge interest in it and it has much wider application than the two that did not survive.

3 Quotes by visionaries about Bitcoin:

"[Bitcoin] is a techno tour de force." - Bill Gates, Founder of Microsoft

"There are three eras of currency: Commodity-based, politically-based, and now, math-based." - Chris Dixon, Internet Entrepreneur and Investor (as quoted by bitcoin.org)

"Bitcoin will do to banks what email did to the postal industry" - Rick Falkvinge, IT Entrepreneur

Obvious all three of these entrepreneurs think that Bitcoin will survive and has a real future.

Alternative Currencies

Alternative currencies are nothing new, so Bitcoin is not revolutionary in that respect. If you lived in Europe in the 1930's you would have seen many communities starting their own currencies in the aftermath of German hyper - inflation and the stock market crash of 1929. In the US in the 1930's there were a plethora of alternative currencies created.

Interestingly, only one of these systems has thrived and has survived until today. It is useful to look at this survivor as it can give us an insight into what is required from an alternative currency to survive long term. Bitcoin will need to meet some of these requirements if it is to secure its longevity.

The Wir

WIR was founded in 1934 by businessmen Werner Zimmermann and Paul Enz as a result of currency shortages and global financial instability. A banking license was granted in 1936 "WIR" is both an abbreviation of Wirtschaftsring and the word for "we" in German, reminding participants that the economic circle is also a community.

The WIR is an independent complementary currency system in Switzerland that serves businesses in hospitality, construction, manufacturing, retail and professional services. WIR issues and manages a private currency, called the WIR Franc, which is used in combination with the Swiss Franc to generate dual-currency transactions.

The WIR Franc is an electronic currency reflected in clients' trade accounts and there is no paper money. WIR has perfected the system by creating a credit system which issues credit, in WIR Francs, to its members. The credit lines are secured by members pledging assets. This ensures that the currency is asset-backed. When two members enter into a transaction with both Swiss Francs and WIR Francs it reduces the amount of cash needed by the buyer; the seller does not discount its product or service.

Although WIR started with only 16 members, today it has grown to include over 62,000. WIR Bank's total assets are approximately 3.0 billion Swiss Francs. The WIR Bank has a stable history, not prone to failure as the current banking system is. It has remained fully operational during times of general economic crisis. The WIR Bank may even dampen downturns in the business cycle, helping to stabilize the Swiss economy during difficult times

Most of us take for granted that the rectangular multi coloured slips of paper we keep in our purses or wallets are the physical embodiment of value. But they are only pieces of paper that we have agreed collectively have a set value. None of the paper or fiat currencies in existence today are backed by gold or any other tangible asset. When you look at it this way, Bitcoin and all the other digital currencies have just as much chance of success as our current monetary systems.

An alternative currency is generally used in conjunction with conventional money. Many attempts at money reform have failed in the past, because they were trying to attack or radically change the official money system itself. Bitcoin is not attacking the official money system per se. What it (currently) does instead is to complement the conventional money system. In November, the U.S Department of Justice said Bitcoins can be "legal means of exchange" at a U.S. Senate committee hearing, boosting prospects for wider acceptance of the virtual currency. "We all recognize that virtual currencies, in and of themselves, are not illegal," Mythili Raman, acting assistant attorney general at the Justice Department's criminal division, said at the hearing.

"The FBI's approach to virtual currencies is guided by a recognition that online payment systems, both centralized and decentralized, offer legitimate financial services," Peter Kadzik, principal deputy assistant attorney general, wrote in a letter dated Oct. 23rd 2013.

These hearings help to bolster the view that Bitcoins are an acceptable alternate means of conducting transactions, and that their use will grow.

Bitcoin is not alone!

Other alternative currencies may be a threat to BitCoin. Since BitCoin was the first virtual currency of its kind, there is always a possibility that BitCoin will be surpassed by another digital currency. There are several available to choose from, including Ripple, LiteCoin , NameCoin, and PPCoin. The latter three are BitCoin based, which means one or more developers downloaded the original BitCoin software files and modified them to create their own virtual currency.

Ripple

BitCoin's closest rival is Ripple, which touts itself as a worldwide open currency and payment system for individuals and businesses. Ripple works off the Ripple Protocol (RTXP) and was created and developed by OpenCoin, Inc. It is made up of three distinct parts, including a payment network, currency exchange centre and Ripple virtual money. It's also an open source program that anyone can take and develop or modify for their own use.

Ripple's primary advantage is they process transactions much faster than BitCoin, which requires a minimum of 10 minutes to verify, secure, and authorize a transaction. Ripple only takes five seconds.

It is also touted as being cheaper than BitCoin. Ripple payments that exclusively use Ripple currency are only charged a security fee of a few cents, which is primarily used as a deterrent to malicious users. Converting the Ripple currency into dollars, pounds, yuans, or any other local currency costs a little more, but that does not affect the seller of Ripple currency. It only affects the receiver when they want to turn their Ripple coins into local cash.

Ripple is an open source program but it is centralized and owned by Ripple Labs. Although Ripple claims to have plans to decentralize the system, this has yet to be seen and the risks are the same with Ripple as they would be with any other centralized currency.

BBQ Coin

BBQ Coin is an alternative currency that appears to be a test currency for individuals looking to get into the digital currency world. This currency allows people to buy BBQ coins and mine for them. BBQ Coin is a fast version of LiteCoin, with 60 second block targets and 42 coins per block. A total of 88 million coins will be mined. Nearly 29 million coins have been created already(at the time of writing). Mining pools available are: Bighhq Pool & BBQ Ltcoin

LiteCoin

LiteCoin was created in 2011 by Coblee and is a spin off from BitCoin's protocols. There are currently $ 60 million worth of LiteCoins circulating. LiteCoin demands that miners show proof-of-work before getting paid. LiteCoin will stop producing coins once it reaches 84 million coins. LiteCoin's claim to fame is its short, 2.5 minute transaction time. Find out more www.litecoin.org

DevCoin

As the name implies, DevCoin is short for Developer Coin. This is touted as the "ethical" crypto currency. It is primarily used by programmers, software developers and writers and was created to help fund open source programming projects. Basically, this is digital currency's crowd-funding coin.

NameCoin

NameCoin was created in 2011. It is also derived from the BitCoin protocols. As Bitcoin frees money, NameCoin frees information access. It allows you to securely register and transfer arbitrary names, attach value to the names and transact NameCoins. There are currently $ 3.8 million worth of coins circulating in the NameCoin network.

PPCoin

PPCoin or Peercoin was created in 2012 by software developer Sunny King, and it is also a fork from the BitCoin protocols. There are currently $ 3.7 million worth of PPCoins circulating on the PPCoin network. This currency requires both a proof-of-work protocol and a proof-of-stake protocol.

The latter was designed to make PPCoin more energy efficient for miners (more proof-of-stake = more PPCoins) and to provide a measure of instant inflation. Unlike Bitcoin there is no hard limit to the number of coins that can be mined. It is designed to eventually attain an annual inflation rate of 15% per annum. This feature aims to allow for longer term scalability.

In Summary

In essence, money is a lifeblood flowing through our society and our global human community.

Money not only has the potential to contribute to global abundance, sustainability and peace of mind if used wisely; but when restricted in its flow it also has the ability to engender immense suffering and extreme hardship. Bitcoin does have the potential to free up the exchange of value on a huge scale as a complementary currency. As long as the Bitcoin does not get railroaded by the speculators and underworld criminal element, it has the potential to help millions of people in third world countries join a digital money system. These millions are currently excluded from the traditional banking system.

As I write, alternative currency startups are being lavishly funded by venture capitalists whilst visionaries gush about the world-changing possibilities of money free from government control. Silicon Valley is of course the natural centre for Bitcoin mania. An advocacy group named Arisebitcoin recently put up 40 billboards around the Bay Area with messages such as: "The Revolution has started? Where do you stand?"

If Bitcoin achieves mass acceptance and adoption, then it really will have caused a revolution!

Appendix:

Technical mining information – only for the tech savvy (many of us will find this section gobbledegook!)

There are two basic ways to mine: On your own or as part of a pool. Almost all miners choose to mine in a pool because it takes the luck out of the process. Before you join a pool, make sure you have a bitcoin wallet so you have a place to store your bitcoins.

Mining pools

Next you need to join a mining pool like Eclipse Mining Consortium, Give Me Coins or BTC Guild. With pool mining, the profit from any block a member generates is divided up among the members of the pool. This gives the pool members a more frequent, steady payout (this is called reducing your variance), but your payout will be less unless you use a zero fee pool like Eclipse. Solo mining will give you large, infrequent payouts, and pooled mining will give you small, frequent payouts, but both add up to the same amount if you're using a zero fee pool.

Once you have your client set up or you have registered with a pool, the next step is to set up the actual mining software. The most popular GPU/FPGA/ASIC miner at the moment is BFGminer or CGminer. If you want a quick taste of mining without installing any software, try Bitcoin Plus, a browser-based CPU Bitcoin miner. As a CPU miner it's not cost-efficient for serious mining, but it does illustrate the principle of pooled mining very well.

During mining, your computer will run a cryptographic hashing function (two rounds of SHA256) on what is called a block header. For each new hash, the mining software will use a different number as the random element of the block header, this number is called the nonce. Depending on the nonce and what else is in the block the hashing function will yield a hash which looks like this:

93ef6f358fbb998c60802496863052290d4c63735b7fe5bdaac821de96a53a9a

You can look at this hash as a really long number. (It's a hexadecimal number, meaning the letters A-F are the digits 10-15.) To make mining even more difficult there is what's called a difficulty target. To create a valid block your miner has to find a hash that is below the difficulty target.

If for example the difficulty target is:

1000000000000000000000000000000000000000000000000000000000,

any number that starts with a zero would be below the target, e.g.:

0787a6fd6e0782f7f8058fbef45f5c17fe89086ad4e78a1520d06505acb4522f

If we lower the target to

0100000000000000000000000000000000000000000000000000000000000000,

we now need two zeros in the beginning to be under it:
00db27957bd0ba06a5af9e6c81226d74312a7028cf9a08fa125e49f15cae4979

Because the target is such an unwieldy number with multiple digits, people generally use a simpler number to express the current target. This number is called the mining difficulty. The mining difficulty expresses how much harder the current block is to generate compared to the first block. So a difficulty of 70000 means to generate the current block you have to do 70000 times more work than Satoshi had to do generating the first block. Back then mining was a lot slower and less optimized. The difficulty changes every 2016 blocks. The network tries to change it such that 2016 blocks at the current global network processing power will take about 14 days. That's why, when the network power rises, the difficulty rises as well.

Bitcoin Mining Hardware

CPU's

In the beginning, mining with a CPU was the only way to mine bitcoins. Mining this way via the original Satoshi client is how the bitcoin network started. Individuals with just a PC could be a miner. This method is no longer viable now that the network difficulty level is so high. You might mine for years and years without earning a single coin.

GPU's

Soon it was discovered that high end graphics cards were much more efficient at bitcoin mining and the landscape changed. CPU bitcoin mining gave way to the GPU (Graphical Processing Unit). The massively parallel nature of some GPUs allowed for a 50x to 100x increase in bitcoin mining power while using far less power per unit of work. While any modern GPU can be used to mine, the AMD line of GPU architecture turned out to be far superior to the nVidia architecture for mining bitcoins and the ATI Radeon HD 5870 turned out to be the most cost effective choice at the time.

FPGA's

CPU transitioned to GPU and both were superseded by the Field Programmable Gate Array. With the successful launch of the Butterfly Labs FPGA 'Single', the bitcoin mining hardware landscape gave way to specially manufactured hardware dedicated to mining bitcoins. A typical FPGA mining device would provide a hashrate of 826 MH/s at 80w of power. That represents a fivefold improvement over the GPU mining power. This made it viable for the first large bitcoin mining farms to be constructed at an operational profit. The bitcoin mining industry was hence born.

ASIC's

Unlike all the previous generations of hardware preceding ASIC, ASIC is the "end of the line" when it comes to disruptive technology. The bitcoin mining world is now solidly in the Application Specific Integrated Circuit (ASIC) era. An ASIC is a chip designed specifically to do one thing and one thing only. Unlike FPGA's, an ASIC cannot be repurposed to perform other tasks. An ASIC designed to mine bitcoins can only mine bitcoins and will only ever mine bitcoins. The inflexibility of an ASIC is offset by the fact that it offers a 100x increase in hashing power while reducing power consumption compared to all the previous technologies. For example, a good bitcoin miner like the Monarch from Butterfly Labs provides 600 GH/s (1 Gigahash is 1000 Megahash. 1 GH/s = 1000 MH/s) while consuming 350w of power. Compared to the GPU era, this is an increase in hash rate and power savings of nearly 300x.

There is nothing on the horizon at the moment to replace ASICs. There will be stepwise refinement of the ASIC products and increases in efficiency, but nothing will offer the 50x - 100x increase in hashing power or 7x reduction in power usage that moves from previous technologies offered. This makes power consumption on an ASIC device the single most important factor of any ASIC product, as the expected useful lifetime of an ASIC mining device is longer than the entire history of bitcoin mining. It is conceivable that an ASIC device purchased today would still be mining in two years if the device is power efficient enough and the cost of electricity does not exceed its output. Mining profitability is also dictated by the exchange rate, but under all circumstances the more power efficient the mining device, the more profitable it is.

Bitcoin mining toolmakers

Many startup companies are racing to design, manufacture, and sell specialized high-performance computers to Bitcoin miners. At the heart of the computers made by HashFast and similar startups such as KnCMiner and Butterfly Labs is the ASIC chip. For Bitcoin-mining toolmakers like HashFast, the goal is to make an ASIC that is precisely tuned to crunch Nakamoto's algorithms. It would take 70,000 of Intel's fastest chips to match one of these new chips.

In August 2013, Texas-based CoinTerra announced two Bitcoin computer designs, which it dubbed GoldStrike and TerraMiner. Ravi Iyengar, a veteran chip designer, runs the startup. Iyengar has worked at Intel, Nvidia, Qualcomm and most recently, Samsung where he led a team that developed chips for the company's phones and tablets. After hearing about Bitcoin, Iyengar quit his job to use his experience to outrace other Bitcoin-mining startups.

The most secretive of the new mining companies is Silicon Valley-based 21e6; its name refers to the scientific notation for 21 million, the maximum number of Bitcoins to be mined. According to regulatory filings, the startup raised $5 million in April 2013 to build what's believed to be one of the fastest mining chips in the world. Among early investors are the Winklevoss twins; Marc Andreessen and his venture capital firm, Andreessen Horowitz; early Tesla Motors backer Bill Lee; PayPal (EBAY) member David Sacks and Naval Ravikant, founder of AngelList, a social network for investors and entrepreneurs.

You can find a really useful comparison chart of the various hardware used in mining rigs here...

https://en.bitcoin.it/wiki/Mining_Hardware_Comparison

Useful links for further reading...

http://pinkinvestments.org/index.php?module=alternative&action=alternative-bitcoin

This is the site that I write content for and a whole segment is devoted to Bitcoin and other alternative investments.

https://www.mtgox.com This is the largest Bitcoin exchange

https://www.bitstamp.net Here you can send Bitcoin over the internet with no middleman.

http://CoinDesk.com   This site averages bitcoin prices across multiple exchanges.

https://coinbase.com/ This site allows you to buy & sell Bitcoin and set up a wallet

http://www.bitcoin.org   This is the home of the original Bitcoin open-source project.

http://www.bitcoinx.com   Here you can find real time quotes from all major Bitcoin exchanges

http://www.blockchain.info   Here you can see data and statistics from the Bitcoin network

https://en.bitcoin.it/wiki/IRC_channels#Communities_for_Exchanges_and_Trading

https://en.bitcoin.it/wiki/Bitcoin-Watch streaming Bitcoin transactions

Bitcoin Wiki -Hundreds of wiki articles on various Bitcoin subjects.Bitcoin related communities

http://www.weusecoins.com/en/merchant-tools Useful info for online merchants